NATIONAL GEOGRAPHIC

T0052324

My Town Used To Be Small

Marvin Buckley

My town used to be small.

Then a big factory opened in my town.
This is what happened.

The big factory needed workers.
New people moved to my town.

workers

The new people needed somewhere to live.
New houses were built in my town.

The people needed to buy things.
New stores were built in my town.

store

The people needed a place to play.
New parks were built in my town.

My town grew and grew.
It's much bigger now.